Let's Talk About It
A Lifestyle Guide

Marsheka Jones

Copyright © 2021 Marsheka Jones
All Rights Reserved. This book and any portion may not be used to reproduced or used in any matter without written and signed permission of the publisher except for brief quotations in a book review.
ISBN: 978-1-7372625-0-3
Author Marsheka Jones

Questionnaire

Do you have trouble sleeping at night?

Do you have life insurance?

Do you have a stable income?

Is your credit score where it needs to be?

Do you own anything of your own?

Are you on a government assistance program?

Is your name constantly being brought up in gossip or drama?

Do you have enough money saved to handle your bills for a year?

Do you hate your job?

Do you eat at fast-food restaurants more than 3 times a week?

Do you exercise?

Is it hard for you to keep relationships with peers?

Have trouble with co-parenting?

Are you constantly picking the wrong people to date?

Do you feel like it is not enough time in a day?

Is your home full of clutter?

Do you cry a lot?

Do you snap off when someone does things you do not like?

Are you a procrastinator?

Prologue

Whatever you are thinking this book is about you are thinking wrong. This is not one of those lifestyle guides that is going to tell you what you want to hear or tiptoe around all the bullshit that is going on in your life to make you feel better. And in no way do I wish to insult anyone, so please don't take things personally. Everything written in this book comes from a loving place and I am working on myself as we speak. This is a lifestyle guide that's going to encourage you to change your fucked up ways, look deep inside of yourself, and be the best you that you can be. And yes, I curse and if you have an issue with that then it is more of a reason you should read this book. You're worried about the wrong shit! Now, I will be the first to admit that I am far from perfect. I use to be all over the place, but with age, time, and hard work I came to realize I can change every situation I encounter. I own up to all my messed-up ways. Whatever your reason, I am glad that you are here reading this today. We are about to go through this journey together. So, grab your pen and let's get started.

Chapter 1
"It's All About Me" Mya feat. Sisqó

Baby hell no, that's not the way it goes, it's all about me tonight

Keeping it real with yourself seems to be the hardest thing for people to do. To move forward and grow you must first be honest about your life and the state it is currently in. Urban people are known for giving themselves so much credit but, our basics are not even together. The first thing we must do is take care of ourselves and that means being real with ourselves. Ask yourself, Am I breathing in clean air? Am I drinking enough water, are the type of foods I am eating well for me? Am I getting enough sleep? Are my sexual needs being met.? The lack of these basic physiological needs is enough to make anyone go crazy. How can you level up in your life if you are not taking care of the basics?

Choosing to practice bad habits and not taking care of yourself can fuck with your life. Now I am not saying you should be some size

0 or cannot have a drink or two. What I am saying is how we take care of ourselves affects everything else in our lives. It is like a domino effect. Eating poorly causes you to have all types of health complications. And how many times have you been told food gives you energy but the first thing you want to do is go your ass to sleep? This is because we are putting the wrong shit in.

Since we are on the subject, let's talk sleep! The lack of sleep can be unhealthy too. I am always less active during the day when I am tired and need more rest. I don't know if it was all the sugary snacks or the pork chop sandwich for dinner, but It has me knocked out for about 4 hours then I'm up the rest of the night which results in a bad morning. I know the struggle is real. There are only 24 hours in a day so who wants to waste 8 hours a day sleeping? Me, that's who! You need all your energy to stay on top of your shit. We need energy for work, we need energy for our children, we need energy for sex, and we need the energy to get that money. If you knew that a few more hours of sleep could benefit you in all these ways, then why not? The goal here is to get into the habit of making better choices with our bodies. This means putting down the car keys sometimes and walking your ass to the store when you need an item or choosing baked instead of fried chicken every once in a while. You only get out of your body what you put into it. Be aware and do better!

Let's Talk About It

Chapter 1 Reflections

Are your basic needs being met?

What are some ways you can improve your health?

What things do you now plan on doing differently to reach your full potential?

Chapter 2
"Triggered" Jhene Aiko

You ruin everything, you do it every time

A lot of people use the term mental health to say they do not have a mental disorder. But to be honest, a lot of you are fucking delusional. The way you think and the way you feel and behave are just all over the place. I've had arguments with people trying to explain that they were cheated on when they were not. What happened was they were being delusional and assuming shit. If You never sat down with the person and agreed that you were in a committed relationship you were not cheated on. Yall were just fucking and going out occasionally. When the other person popped up in a relationship, you were heartbroken, played the victim, and overreacted. You played yourself!

Communication is key! You should've made it known you wanted a relationship. And if they weren't on the same page, you should've moved the fuck around. No one is holding a gun to your head forcing you to do anything. When you communicate your expectations, it helps hold others accountable for their actions; But the missed management of emotions and the poor thinking of people today are becoming so bad that it is now affecting relationships, daily routines, and our health. If you never heard the song Triggered by Jhene Aiko, then I need you to. It is the perfect song to show how a lot of us are mentally fucked up and how being mentally unstable can influence our life. From the title, you can already guess what the song is about, but I need you to pay attention to what's going on. In this song, which was written by Brian Warfield, Jhene Aiko, Julian Quan Viet Le, Maclean Robinson, and Ross O'donoghue; Jhene Aiko sings "Maybe I'm overreacting. Baby I don't know what happened. You know all my bad habits you know it's hard for me to control that shit, cause when I get mad, I get big mad". Reacting poorly on things before getting all the facts is a dangerous game to play. This is what I like to call rollercoaster vibes. This happens when You can't manage your emotions; so, one minute you are calm and the next you're ready to blow someone's head off and hurt yourself while doing it (Damn Dummies).

All this toxic energy can be fixed if you just stop putting yourself in situations where you may have to act like anything other than the king or queen that you are. If you know that you are going to pop off after going through your significant other's phone, then DON'T DO IT! If you know that being in a relationship is not for you then DON'T be in one. And If you don't know all the facts then don't assume anything. You must teach yourself that whether it is the people, places, or things if it is messing with your mind then "fuck it"! But you also need to realize sometimes it's not them, it's you!

Let's Talk About It
Chapter 2 Reflections

What are your triggers? (Things that is mood-altering that may cause an undesirable reaction):

Recall a time where you overreacted, what happened?

What are some of your bad habits?

Chapter 3
"It's A Vibe" by 2Chainz feat. Ty Dolla $ign, & Trey Songz

VIBE IS THE REALEST, I KNOW YOU FEEL IT...

A person's aura is everything. It is often what unconsciously attracts people to us. Imagine a person entering your room, they seem calm and unbothered, they smell pleasant, they look well-rested, and this person makes you feel welcomed and at ease. These traits show a person who cares for themselves and carries a good aura. But to create a good aura you must always protect your energy. Protecting your energy means you must let shit go without letting people walk over you and mistreat you. No one deserves to be subject to abuse. But instead of overreacting choose your battles. It's okay to bite your tongue If it means you won't have to raise your voice or say something you may not mean during an argument.

To create a good aura, you must work on yourself and how you handle situations. Limit toxic exposure and be aware of the people you allow in your life. When trying to keep a good vibe, especially after being upset, try a self-redirection exercise. Meditation is a great way to refocus your energy and calm yourself down. Begin by sitting in a quiet space and breathe slowly. Even music can be mood-altering. Keeping good energy is our number one goal.

A lot of people don't realize this but sometimes the things you hold on to can throw off your vibes. Clean up your personal space and your social media. Many things can hold bad vibes and memories which can cause you to have a bad aura. Maybe it's the picture hanging on your wall that your toxic ex bought you or the comforter set that you kept from that depressed ass roommate. Whatever the item, get rid of it. Cutting back from social media is good as well. If you can't resist, then try filling your timeline with people of value. Inspirational things, funny videos, and supportive friends.

The Train Ride

Items and social media are not the only things that should be cut out or limited. It is the people too. We love to believe that people we consider family and friends are ride or die and have good intentions for us, but a lot of times they don't. Think of your life as a train. The people on the train with you seem to be going in the same direction, but remember a train has many stops. Some people get on, others get off, and only a few will stay on the train to the very end. You are the conductor and only you can choose the people you want on the train. Of course, these people may not stay until the end, but you may come across a few people that can bring what you need to help you get to that destination. Maybe you took a wrong turn, and a passenger has a map, or you break down along the way and someone has the tools you need to get back on track. Ultimately the choice is yours. You can bring along whatever you please and you also have the power to leave things behind.

Example: Meet Renae

Renae is the conductor of her train which symbolizes this thing called life. On the train is Renae's 2 children. Her children will ride with her on this train until they decide to leave to go in a direction of their own. Renae also has her children's father Jace, who is also on the train. Jace helps protect and care for their children but often leaves the train to care for his other children. Since Renae and Jace are not married, Jace's other children are not a part of Renae's train even though they are a part of her children's train. Renae also has her parents and siblings on her train, this is her immediate family. They have a lot of influence on the type of person Renae is and they have transfer passes that allow them to board Renae's train when she needs a break from time to time. Renae has a few friends that board the train. Some of these friends are there to look out the window and enjoy the view while others keep her sane during what seems to be the everlasting train ride. Eventually, someone will get on the train and stay on to the very end. This may be a spouse, a lifelong friend, or a close family member.

Let's Talk About It
Chapter 3 Reflection
Describe your train scenario.

Chapter 4
"C. R. E. A. M." Wu-Tang Clan

*Cash Rules Everything Around Me CREAM get the money,
Dolla Dolla bill yall!*

Let's talk money. Are you financially stable? It's time to start preparing yourself for the lifestyle that you want to live. If money, cars, clothes, and a lavish life are the things you desire then you must know how to go get it. But you will never receive that can of success if your basics are not in order. Being financially stable for yourself and your family is the first key. Most of the time people know how to get the money, keeping the money is where people fall short. The first thing people need to realize is that they don't have it like they say they do. Be honest with yourself about what you got going on with your finances. What do you have going for yourself for you to live comfortably? Is your money working for you? Are you living paycheck to paycheck? Are your children taken care of? How much money do you have saved? Do you have a retirement plan? Do you have a valid source of income? Do you have life insurance? And is the money you're bringing in monthly enough to cover all your expenses? For example, if you make $3000 a month is that enough to afford a $600 a month car note, $1300 a month on rent, utilities, food, childcare cost, internet, and enough to maintain your upkeep? Probably not.

You must be realistic with yourself and make some changes to get to where you want to be. A lot of people are chasing a bag but when will the time come when we stop chasing the bag and let the bag chase us? It's time to take money seriously. Start by cutting the unnecessary spending. There's no way you should be rocking the latest fashions if you are two months behind on your mortgage payments. Learn how to create a budget where you can have money left over to invest in things that will double your money instead of using it for bullshit. Now, I'm not saying you shouldn't use your money for occasional pleasures, I'm saying make more than you spend. When you are in grind mode everything you do should bring value to you. You want money coming in from all directions. Your job shouldn't be your only source of income because you can lose a job today and they will replace you tomorrow. Find yourself a side hustle. Pick up a skill that you can make money from. There are so many things you can do to make extra money from washing cars to cutting hair. The ways to make extra money is endless. Don't be that flashy person who doesn't have their shit together. Be about your shit and let your money talk for you.

Let's Talk About It

Chapter 4 Reflection

Simple Budgeting

Money Out

Expense	Amount
Housing (Rent, Mortgage, Taxes, Home Insurance)	_____
Utilities (Electricity, Gas, Water, Trash, Internet)	_____
Transportation (Car Note, Insurance, Ride Share)	_____
Groceries	_____
Personal Care	_____
Child Care	_____
Other	_____
Total	_____

Money In

Expense	Amount
Paycheck	_____
Additional Income	_____
Other	_____
Total	_____

Money Left Over

Money in minus Money Out	_____

Chapter 5
"Thankful" DJ Khaled feat. Lil Wayne & Jeremih

Be proud, be shameless, be now, be ancient

The desire to be the best you that you can be lives deep inside of self. The level of self-actualization is achievable if you take accountability for the state your life is in right now and work on bettering yourself. What matters is you! After a certain age, none of the bullshit matters anymore. What matters in life is making sure your basic needs are met if you feel safe and secure with yourself and in your relationships and getting everything that your heart desires.

Start working on yourself today. Don't wait until the clock stops ticking or procrastinate another year. Start today! Get yourself a journal so you can let all those emotions you have bottled up out; don't let yourself be seen as angry or bitter because you choose to express your emotions to the wrong people. Get a goal book, that way you will be able to keep track of the things you want to accomplish in life.

Keep yourself busy. When you occupy your time doing things that bring you peace you don't have time for all the other bullshit. Staying busy means you won't have time to be stalking your partners every move or entertaining gossip.

Whether you are starting from the bottom or already got life figured out, make sure that you do it gracefully. Don't be afraid to fuck up or start all over. It's your life to live. The views and opinions of others are none of your business. Be proud that you dared to take the first steps. And if you fail, fuck it, at least you tried. Life begins and ends with you!

Message to my son

Son, you are my biggest flex. Baby boy If you don't know now, I hope you soon learn that you are simply worthy. You deserve to be recognized. You deserve to live a long, beautiful life and you deserve to be happy. You will be respected as a man and a wonderful member of society. One day you're going to accomplish great things and I hope it is God's will to be with you every step of the way in your journey in life. If I could explain the joy I feel just from having you as my son, it would be another 10 chapters in my book. Son, be the best that you can be! Go after your dreams, take care of your responsibilities, be a man of your word, and respect life. I love you forever and a day Mazir!

Love Mommy

www.ingramcontent.com/pod-product-compliance
Lightning Source LLC
LaVergne TN
LVHW071031070426
835507LV00002B/115